REVEALED

A Christian Understanding for Celebrating
the Biblical Holidays of Rosh Hashanah and Yom Kippur

BY KENNETH S. ALBIN

HIDDEN BLESSINGS REVEALED

A Christian Understanding for Celebrating the Biblical Holidays of Rosh Hashanah and Yom Kippur.

BY

KENNETH S. ALBIN

For more information about Kenneth S. Albin

www.hitthemarktv.com
www.savethenations.com

TABLE OF CONTENTS

DESCRIPTIONS

WHAT ARE THE MOEDIM?

The Moedim are appointed days, rehearsals and special set times that God invites His people to gather as a congregation to meet with Him, their Creator and King. In God's sovereignty He has chosen, from the beginning of creation, seven appointed times during His calendar year.

WHAT IS THE SABBATH?

God has also, in His sovereignty, chosen another day that is set apart from the rest. God has pre-determined, by His sovereignty, to set apart the seventh day as the Sabbath for man to rest and to honor the Creator. The Sabbath was created for all of mankind, not just the Jew, Israel, but for all mankind.

WHAT IS A CHRISTIAN?

The word Christian is mentioned three times in the New Testament. It is the Greek word Christianos. The term means "to be a little Christ" or "anointed". The term is used to point to a true disciple of Jesus Christ. A Christian is committed to following Jesus Christ, His teachings, His ways and His commands. The disciple of Christ will become more and more like Jesus as the Holy Spirit continues to work and conform their lives to the will of God. A real Christian has been born again and passed from death to life and darkness to the kingdom of Light. (Acts 11:26, Acts 26:28, 1 Peter 4:16, John 5:24, Colossians 1:13,)

WHO ARE THE JEWS?

The word Jew is a term used to describe those from the Southern Kingdom, tribe of Judah or the house of Judah. A Jew may also be from the tribe of Benjamin since that was the tribe given to David's descendants by the prophet Ahijah when he divided the two kingdoms and gave ten tribes to Jeroboam and two tribes to Solomon's son, Rehoboam. In the Southern Kingdom of Judah there were also some from the tribe of Levi and remnants of other tribes. These would also be known as being Jews or Jewish. The Northern Kingdom with ten tribes became commonly known as the house of Israel.

WHAT IS A GENTILE?

The term Gentile comes from the Hebrew word Goy or its plural Goyim. It refers to the nations who were not physical descendants of Israel. A Gentile can also be used of the house of Israel, sometimes known as Ephraim, who lost their inheritance and identity when they, in their apostasy and divorce from Yahweh, were scattered to the nations, never to return. They are commonly referred to as the lost tribes of Israel. When a person accepts Jesus, he is "grafted-in" to Israel and becomes connected to and a descendant of Abraham by faith. It is important to understand that a Christian and follower of Jesus is no longer a Gentile. (2 Kings 17:23, Ephesians 2:11-19)

WHAT IS A HEBREW?

A Hebrew is the term meaning "one from beyond" or "crossed over one". It refers to Abram who crossed over the Euphrates River into a land that was promised by the God who revealed Himself as the true and living God. Abram crossed over spiritually to forsake his father's idols and worship El Shaddai.

WHAT IS A HEBREW CHRISTIAN?

Though the term is not common or usually connected, it should be. A Christian is a person who has crossed over from death to life and from darkness to light. This person is a disciple of Jesus Christ and follows His teachings.

A Hebrew Christian is a person who also embraces their inheritance and identity in connection to Abraham. The Hebrew Christian understands that they are not separated from, but connected to Israel, and receives the benefits of that rich tree and identity.

In no way is a Christian or a Hebrew Christian ever to think they replace natural Israel or the Jewish people. This is a dangerous and demonic doctrine that has caused many to horrors in the past. The Hebrew Christian is no longer hacked and no longer has their identity and inheritance stolen. They begin to see the Shalom of God working mightily "Nothing Missing, Nothing Broken, Nothing Lost, All Restored!"

WHAT IS TORAH?

Most commonly this refers to the first five books of the Bible known as the Pentateuch. The Torah can also refer to the entire Old Testament known as the Tanakh. Many think it means "law" or a book of "do's and don'ts", but this incorrect. The truest understanding of Torah is "instruction and teaching". The root word for Torah is yarah and it is an archery term meaning, "to hit the mark".

Throughout the Scriptures the promise of good things, life and well-being is connected and given to those who obey Torah. The New Testament word for sin means "to miss the mark". So when we obey Torah we "hit the mark" and live well, but when we sin by disobeying the Torah we get the consequences. The Torah, God's Voice and God's Word are all synonymous. (Deuteronomy 4:40, 5:29, Proverbs 6:23, Psalm 119:105)

INTRODUCTION:

It is with great anticipation and joy that I have written this book for you to read. I might not know you personally, but I am aware that another spiritual awakening is happening in our midst. You have been hearing and heeding the call and the Spirit's drawing. He has been calling you deeper to learn and experience the roots and foundations for the faith and the Way of the Lord.

The early church was known simply as "The Way". The Holy Spirit was instructing, leading and guiding the disciples in the footsteps of Messiah, Yeshua-Jesus, who was alive in His people and through them continued His ministry of preaching, teaching and demonstrating the Kingdom. The book of Acts was a new beginning and something we can learn and draw understanding from still today.

Since what we call the New Testament wasn't written or compiled yet, we know that the Early Church only had the written Revelation of the Old Testament as its foundation for the faith. The richness of God's instruction and revelation are found in its pages and will later be confirmed by the New Testament. They together as God's revealed word will be a seamless masterpiece of the oracles of God that complement and confirm one another over and over.

There is something you can receive and learn in the "now" and "present season" of our lives, as well as prophetic connections to past and future events, that are in the Moedim of the Lord. They are pointers and God's gift to us to show us set times, rehearsals and His Divine appointments.

Genesis 1:14 GW
Then God said, "Let there be lights in the sky to separate the day from the night. They will be signs (Moedim) and will mark religious festivals, days, and years.

It's hard for us to understand how, before man arrived, that God would have already had this in place, but the plans and purposes of God for each one of us have already been written in the books of heaven. When we learn about and begin to keep these appointed times, we begin to align ourselves with the plan and book He has for each one of us.

Jesus came to do the will of the Father of what was written in His book. (Psalm 40:7, Hebrews 10:7). Jesus understood that He was also connected to the seasons and times of God. The first coming of Messiah had confirmations in all of the Moedim feasts that occur in our springtime. Jesus died on the Passover, was buried just before the Sabbath of the Feast of Unleavened Bread, was raised on the first fruits of the barley and on Pentecost He gave the Holy Spirit who came to dwell in the disciples and write the Torah-Word on their hearts. So, if Jesus first coming coincided with these springtime Feasts, could His second coming coincide with the three that remain in the fall?

The Apostle Paul wrote that the feasts are shadows of the future, so we know they are very important as they signal and indicate a time in the future for all of creation. In this book Hidden Blessings Revealed you will learn about the first two of the fall feasts and how they are greatly connected and are an important part of a prophetic timeline that has to do with Messiah Jesus' coming again. If you want to know more about all of the Moedim, I challenge you to read my other books on each of the Spring and Fall Feasts to learn how each one has meaning and blessings for now and the future. It is my desire to help you walk out the hidden revelations and practical applications of God's Appointed times in faith and the power of the Holy Spirit.

One of the things we must relearn is how the early church celebrated these Moedim. Even though they had people born as native Jews and those born from the nations, they all did the same thing when it came to worship and living the ways of the Lord. They both kept all the Feasts of the Lord because these are not a salvation issue but one of alignment and blessing. Again I like to say, you don't have to, but you get to! The secret is that once you begin to do them I promise you will really want to keep them as well. They will become a confirmation and rehearsal for what is and what is to come!

The Apostle Paul, as he traveled to the different churches on his missionary journeys, made sure they were all taught the same instructions. He wanted his letter read and passed to each church so they would all get the same teaching and understanding about what they were all to do. As you read the Word with this lens you will have a new picture of the early church as a prototype of all believers in Yeshua-Jesus worshiping and keeping the Feasts of the Lord and the Sabbaths in childlike obedience as a confirmation of their faith.

Colossians 4:16 NIV
16 After this letter has been read to you, see that it is also read in the church of the Laodiceans and that you in turn read the letter from Laodicea.

1 Thessalonians 5:27 NIV
27 I charge you before the Lord to have this letter read to all the brothers and sisters.

The Apostle Paul also sent his spiritual son and disciple, Timothy to take the letters and the teachings as a standard in every church. So if we can find just one of the churches doing these things it would have been all of them. Also, the early church had only the Old Testament or what the Hebrews called the Tanakh as the scriptures they were following. They all knew that Jesus did not loosen or destroy these, for in them was life and light for all.

1 Corinthians 4:17 AMP
17 For this very cause I sent to you Timothy, who is my beloved and trustworthy child in the Lord, who will recall to your minds my methods of proceeding and course of conduct and way of life in Christ, such as I teach everywhere in each of the churches.

1 Corinthians 4:17 YLT
17 because of this I sent to you Timotheus, who is my child, beloved and faithful in the Lord, who shall remind you of my ways in Christ, according as everywhere in every assembly I teach.

As we look at the first two of the fall feasts, I hope and pray the eyes of your understanding would be enlightened and you would know what is the hope of His calling and the riches of the glory of His inheritance in each of His people. I believe there are untold spoils and treasures waiting for us to uncover and unveil.

Let's begin!

CHAPTER ONE:

A New Beginning!

When I think about Rosh Hashanah, which means the "head of the year" in Hebrew, I immediately think about a new beginning and a fresh start. The Hebrew calendar has locked in it a civil or agricultural new year, and a spiritual new year. The springtime is when Passover was instituted and God himself made it the first month. Originally the month was called Abib. The spring feasts begin the spiritual New Year. The fall feasts are also a new beginning, but they represent the physical birthdays.

If you are born again you can probably tell me your spiritual and physical birthdays and they are not going to be the same dates. It is with this in mind that we learn from the rabbis who believe the physical birthday of the world was on Rosh Hashanah. This would be the first day of the physical creation when God spoke the world into existence by His Word and the Holy Spirit. We must understand how interconnected we are with God's creation, for He created the world first before He created Adam and Eve to enjoy, rule over, protect and be sustained by its abundant resources.

In Leviticus chapter twenty-three you will find all seven of the Moedim and the Sabbath as a framework and guideline to govern our time and seasons in relationship with Yahweh. These are also all meant to be a blessing and a picture of what is to come. I have found out that these appointed times, whether in the fall or the springtime, are what God has chosen to use to help us grow in our faith. Just as many fruits and plants grow the most in the spring and the fall. We also do our best growing in the Lord during these appointed times. God also gives us the physical world and these times to understand and connect with the unseen spiritual world. Even the celebration of these times releases something powerful in our lives and the atmosphere is charged with faith for miracles. By saying yes to these times and by beginning to do them, you will see life and blessings flow like never before. Let's read about the first fall feasts.

Leviticus 23:23-25 NKJV
23 Then the Lord spoke to Moses, saying, 24 "Speak to the children of Israel, saying: 'In the seventh month, on the first day of the month, you shall have a sabbath-rest, a memorial of blowing of trumpets, a holy convocation. 25 You shall do no customary work on it; and you shall offer an offering made by fire to the Lord.' "

According to Leviticus, the first day of the seventh month is to be a very significant time, for it is a day you have a special Sabbath, a special offering, a special holy assembly and a special memorial of blowing the trumpets. This day is actually more biblically called "Yom Teruah", which is Hebrew for "day of the blowing of the trumpets." When we begin to look at it with this term in mind, it will take on a much greater significance and help us see it very present in the New Testament church teachings.

There are ten days from when the trumpet at Yom Teruah is to be blown at the first day of the seventh month and when another appointed time, known as the Day of Atonement, is celebrated. The days that are in between these two appointments are connecting the two holy days. They are called the Days of Awe and also known as Teshuvah, which means "to turn or repent" in Hebrew. God in His mercy always will give an opportunity and gift of repentance for us when we fall short of His glory. Since ten is the number that can represent judgment, these days are pointing to something, to a time to come, which will culminate on the Day of Atonement.

During these times the trumpets call us with each blast and sound to a new beginning, a turning from the past, and call us to go higher in our walk with Yahweh. We can see this as we study how the silver trumpets are made.

Numbers 10: -1-2 LB
Now the Lord said to Moses, "Make two trumpets of beaten (hammered-beaten out of one piece,), silver to

be used for summoning the people to assemble and for signaling the breaking of camp.

The silver trumpets were to be made of hammered and beaten silver from one solid piece. The beating of the silver speaks of how our lives must be "hammered" by God's Word as it continues to form us into the image of Christ. The process of being molded into shape by hammering is one that is painful for our flesh. We know that Jesus was beaten as the silver and proved His righteousness, for He walked without sin. When we keep this time, we too will become a trumpet that has been hammered and formed and the Holy Spirit's wind will blow through us and move in us in power!

When we celebrate Rosh Hashanah we are identifying with the price He paid for us to have our positional right, standing with God, and the honor of allowing His Word to conform us to His image and likeness.

This will be happening spiritually to us on Yom Teruah as we are reminded to turn away from the ways of Egypt and the love for the world, and to be ready to meet Christ when He comes. The connection of the physical and spiritual will come together for us in a special way at this time. His Word will mold and shape us like silver to become a voice and trumpet for the Lord.

Jeremiah 23:29
Is not my word like as a fire? saith the LORD; and like a hammer that breaketh the rock in pieces?

Silver is the symbol for righteousness and is very important. It is a precious metal and soft enough to be shaped into whatever the maker desires. The tabernacle pillars were all connected by silver.

Malachi 3:3 NIV
"He will sit as a refiner and purifier of silver; he will purify the Levites and refine them like gold and silver. Then the LORD will have men who will bring offerings in righteousness"

We believers have two kind of righteousness; one is positional and received by faith with childlike humility. 2 Corinthians 5:21 teaches us that we get the Lord Our Righteousness when we exchange our sinful lives for the grace and mercy that only comes through Messiah and His blood.

The other type of righteousness is choosing to live in full obedience out of love and empowered by grace. I like to say this is practical righteousness and how we walk out by faith and the Holy Spirit as a proof and confirmation of our love for the Lord. They are like two sides of a coin we need the positional and the practical to really get the full scope and understanding of the power in righteousness.

Many Christians today aren't aware that the Scriptures are given to instruct us in our righteousness. This is the way we live as one who lives in honor, love and obedience as confirmation and testimony of our faith. Jesus told us to "go and make disciples, teaching them to obey all I command." (Matthew 28)

Revelation 19:7-8
7 Let us be glad and rejoice and give Him glory, for the marriage of the Lamb has come, and His wife has made herself ready." 8 And to her it was granted to be arrayed in fine linen, clean and bright, for the fine linen is the righteous acts of the saints.

Psalm 18:20 HCSB
The LORD rewarded me according to my righteousness; He repaid me according to the cleanness of my hands.

Psalm 58:11 NKJV
11 So that men will say, "Surely there is a reward for the righteous; Surely He is God who judges in the earth."

Matthew 10:41 NKJV
He who receives a prophet in the name of a prophet shall receive a prophet's reward. And he who receives a righteous man in the name of a righteous man shall receive a righteous man's reward.

Take a look at this parable that Jesus taught that has to do with this prophetic time of the year.

Matthew 25:1-13 NLT
"Then the Kingdom of Heaven will be like ten bridesmaids who took their lamps and went to meet the bridegroom. 2 Five of them were foolish, and five were wise. 3 The five who were foolish didn't take enough olive oil for their lamps, 4 but the other five were wise enough to take along extra oil. 5 When the bridegroom was delayed, they all became drowsy and fell asleep.
6 "At midnight they were roused by the shout, 'Look, the bridegroom is coming! Come out and meet him!'
7 "All the bridesmaids got up and prepared their lamps.
8 Then the five foolish ones asked the others, 'Please give us some of your oil because our lamps are going out.' 9 "But the others replied, 'We don't have enough for all of us. Go to a shop and buy some for yourselves.' 10 "But while they were gone to buy oil, the bridegroom came. Then those who were ready went in with him to the marriage feast, and the door was locked.11 Later, when the other five bridesmaids returned, they stood outside, calling, 'Lord! Lord! Open the door for us!' 12 "But he called back, 'Believe me, I don't know you!' 13 "So you, too, must keep watch! For you do not know the day or hour of my return.

The five virgins who were not prepared had not been processed. They got sleepy when the bridegroom did not come as expected. They did not have enough of their own oil filling their lamps. They wanted the other virgins to give their oil.

Five of the virgins were like the silver trumpets that had been hammered and molded into shape, but the five foolish virgins did not think they needed the turning and repentance. They had not prepared through Teshuvah and were not ready for the Bridegroom's return.

Each person must have their own oil and go through a personal journey and process. There are some things that can only be processed as the silver is molded and shaped intentionally through beating into shape. Our will must humble itself to submit and be present in the process. The time being molded and beaten may not be pleasant, but afterward the reward is great. This moulding and shaping by God's Word and the Holy Spirit comes as we seek Him and ask the Spirit to do His work. Ask the Lord is there anything in my life that heaven can't live with? If Heaven can't live with it then it is time to lay it down at the altar. This is a process that really begins as the awakening blast of the shofar is calling us to go hider and to enter into a time of repentance and new beginnings.

The first day of the seventh month is a new beginning and a preparation for something to come. In the next chapter we will look at some Hidden Blessings Revealed in this appointed time.

CHAPTER ONE:

Personal or Small Group Study

What do we learn from the rabbis that Rosh Hashanah is?

____

____

____

These ___________________ times, whether in the fall or the springtime, are what God has chosen to use to help us ___________ in our faith.

Genesis 1:14 GW
Then God said, "Let there be ___________________
in the sky to separate the day from the night. They will be signs (___________________) and will mark ___________________ festivals, days, and years.

God also gives us the _________________ world and
these__________________________ to understand and connect
with the ____________________ spiritual world.

Even the celebration of these times ___________
something powerful in our lives and the
_________________ is charged with __________ for
miracles.

What is the term for the days between the first two holy
days of the seventh month?
____

What is Teshuvah?

____
____
____
____

What is the number that can represent judgment?

____

The _______________ call us with each blast and sound
to a new _______________, turning from the
___________________, and call us to go ___________ in
our walk with Yahweh.

The _______________ trumpets were to make of
_______________ and beaten _________________________ from
one solid piece.

The _____________________of the silver speaks of how
our lives must be _____________________________ by
God's Word as it continues to form us into the image of
Christ.

Silver is the symbol for _____________________________ and
is very important. It is a precious metal and
_____________________________ enough to be _______________
into whatever the maker desires.

Describe the two types of righteousness?

____

____

____

____

____

____

____

____

____

____

There are some things that can only be ______________ as the silver is molded and shaped ______________ through ______________ into shape.

CHAPTER TWO:

Are You Ready?

So you might be thinking, "Hey, what does the Rapture have to do with the Rosh Hashanah and Feast of Trumpets season?" Do you remember it was Paul who talked about in Colossians that these feasts are shadows of the future? (Colossians 2:17) What did he mean by that?

The Colossian church was challenged by the culture and religion of the ascetics who told them not to keep God's appointments, but Paul boldly told the church "Do not let them influence you for they (*God's Feasts*) are shadows and point to a reality in the future." Does not a shadow prove that something real is there? Please don't discount or disregard these days in your life for they are a key that connects you to the destiny and book written about your life. These are what the Greek calls "Kairos " moments and if the devil Himself wants to and would try to challenge and change them you better believe he knows they mean something big!

So what does Yom Teruah point to? It points to the Rapture and "catching away" of the Bride of Christ and goes along with the parable of the ten virgins we read about in the last chapter from Matthew twenty-five. Although the term rapture isn't in the Bible, we can see it throughout Scripture as a day that God will come and "catch away" His bride.

The term "to catch away" is a marital term. The tribe of Benjamin would go yearly to "catch themselves a bride."

Enoch was "caught away" and brought to be with the Lord for God took him after walking with God for hundreds of years.

Elijah the prophet was "caught away" by the Spirit of the Lord in a whirlwind and chariots of fire.

So, why would we say that this feast points to the Rapture?

The word Teruah actually means "to make a loud noise or a shout." It is believed that Adam awoke and declared Yahweh as his King. Rosh Hashanah is the day on which kings were coroneted or set and crowned as kings. It is also known as Hamelech, "the king".

The rabbis also believed that this is the time the gates are opened in heaven.

- TRUMPETS CALL US TO GATHER TO GOD AND TO GET AND BE READY.

- THE TRUMPETS CALLED THE PEOPLE TO MEET WITH GOD ON SINAI

- THE TRUMPETS SOUNDED FOR BATTLES LIKE JERICHO

- THE TRUMPET SOUNDED IN REVELATION TO CALL JOHN TO COME UP HIGHER

Joshua 6:1-5 NKJV

Now Jericho was securely shut up because of the children of Israel; none went out, and none came in. 2 And the Lord said to Joshua: "See! I have given Jericho into your hand, its king, and the mighty men of valor. 3 You shall march around the city, all you men of war; you shall go all around the city once. This you shall do six days. 4 And seven priests shall bear seven trumpets of rams' horns before the ark. But the seventh day you shall march around the city seven times, and the priests shall blow the trumpets. 5 It shall come to pass, when they make a long blast with the ram's horn, and when you hear the sound of the trumpet, that all the people shall shout (Teruah) with a great shout (Teruah); then the wall of the city will fall down flat. And the people shall go up every man straight before him."

When Joshua and the people shouted (Teruah), the walls came down! Yom Teruah is a New Beginning for you and as you shout and keep this celebration, walls are going to come down. Walls that have kept you from possessing spiritual and physical territory are coming down. Doors that have been inaccessible to you will be opened and you will walk through them as they open for you.

Numbers 10:9-10
9 "When you go to war in your land against the enemy who oppresses you, then you shall sound an alarm (loud noise) with the trumpets, and you will be remembered before the Lord your God, and you will be saved from your enemies. 10 Also in the day of your gladness, in your appointed feasts, and at the beginning of your months, you shall blow the trumpets over your burnt offerings and over the sacrifices of your peace offerings; and they shall be a memorial for you before your God: I am the Lord your God."

The trumpets are a natural way to connect with the Lord. He promised to remember and rescue His people for they remind God of His covenant and the sound of the trumpet should wake you up to remember that you have a covenant with the Lord sealed with the blood of Jesus!

The sound of the trumpet is a wake up call to worship, to war and to repent. The trumpet at this time reminds us to examine ourselves, to repent and to calibrate our will to God's will. This trumpet also reminds us that Jesus is coming back and we must be ready and not be asleep and without oil like the five foolish virgins. The Lord, at the Rapture, is going to come with a shout of the Teruah and "catch away" His Bride.

1 Thessalonians 5:16-18 NLT
16 For the Lord himself will come down from heaven with a commanding shout, with the voice of the archangel, and with the trumpet call of God. First, the believers who have died will rise from their graves. 17 Then, together with them, we who are still alive and remain on the earth will be caught up in the clouds to meet the Lord in the air. Then we will be with the Lord forever. 18 So encourage each other with these words.

1 Corinthians 15:51 NKJV
51 Behold, I tell you a mystery: We shall not all sleep, but we shall all be changed— 52 in a moment, in the twinkling of an eye, at the last trumpet. For the trumpet will sound, and the dead will be raised incorruptible, and we shall be changed. 53 For this corruptible must put on incorruption, and this mortal must put on immortality. 54 So when this corruptible has put on incorruption, and this mortal has put on immortality, then shall be brought to pass the saying that is written: "Death is swallowed up in victory."

The last trumpet refers to Rosh Hashanah and Yom Teruah. The believers were aware that this was a time for us to expect Messiah to come and catch away His Bride. As you keep this time you are aware of Christ as your Husband and how He wants to catch you away to be with Him. This is a time of comfort and expectancy. This is a time that we seek to be ready to meet Him when He comes!

Titus 2:11-14 TLV
11 For the grace of God has appeared, bringing salvation to all men, 12 training us to deny ungodliness and worldly desires and to live in a manner that is self-controlled and righteous and godly in the present age. 13 We wait for the blessed hope and appearance of the glory of our great God and Savior, Messiah Yeshua. 14 He gave Himself for us so that He might redeem us from every lawless deed and so that He might purify for Himself a chosen people, zealous for good deeds.

Numbers 23:19-21
19 "God is not a man, that He should lie, Nor a son of man, that He should repent. Has He said, and will He not do? Or has He spoken, and will He not make it good? 20 Behold, I have received a command to bless; He has blessed, and I cannot reverse it. 21 "He has not observed iniquity in Jacob, Nor has He seen wickedness in Israel. The Lord his God is with him, And the shout (Teruah) of a King is among them.

As we close this chapter, don't be afraid of keeping or talking about these feasts of the Lord, for they are not just for Israel or something that was done in the past. The reality is that in keeping them you are connecting to a future day when Christ will come as our worthy Husband and Groom to catch us away to our mansion in our Father's house. He is preparing for you, so it's time for us to be prepared for Him. Don't be caught asleep and unprepared without oil, but use these times in the physical to connect with the spiritual. Are you ready? Are you making the preparations to be in sync with God's timeline and calendar? This is God's way for all of His kids.

Now, let's look and see how we can bridge into the next fall feast that begins on the tenth of the seventh month. There's so much revelation revealed I can hardly wait for it!

CHAPTER TWO:

Personal and Small Group Study

Do you remember it was Paul who talked about in Colossians that these ________________ are ________________ of the future?

The word Teruah actually means "to make a loud ________ or a ________________."

What are at least four things the blowing of the trumpets will be for?

1.______________________________________

____

____

2.______________________________________

____

____

3.______________________________________

____

____

4.____

____

____

What event does Yom Teruah point to that is in the
future?

____

____

____

What is a way to describe the word Rapture?

______________ ______________

Give three biblical references to what we call the
Rapture?
1.____

____

____

2.____

____

____

3.____

____

____

Rosh Hashanah is the day on which ___________ were ___________________ or set and ____________ as kings.

The rabbis also believed that this is the time the _________________ are opened in __________________.

The sound of the trumpet is a wake up call to ____________, to _________ and to _______________.

The trumpet at this time reminds us to ___________________ ourselves, ______________and to _________________ our will to God's will.

This trumpet also reminds us that ____________ is coming back and we must be ______________and not _________ and ________________________like the five foolish virgins.

1 Thessalonians 5:16-18 NLT
16 For the Lord himself will come down from heaven with a commanding ________________, with the ____________ of the archangel, and with the _______________call of God. First, the ___________________ who have died will rise from their graves. 17 Then, together with them, we who are still alive and remain on the earth will be ____________

27

______ in the ____________ to meet the Lord in the
____________. Then we will be with the Lord forever. 18
So ______________ each other with these words.

As you keep this time, you are aware of ______________
as your ______________ and how He wants to ________
you away to be with ________.

CHAPTER THREE:

The Rapture!

One of the questions that come up when anyone begins to predict that Jesus will come at a certain time is a Scripture from the words of Jesus. Although I have heard of people who have done this to their own demise, I am not advocating, endorsing or condoning this for it is not wise.

The Word of God and the Moedim are part of the timeline of heaven and is a part of the way the Holy Spirit will use to direct us on our journey as He uses them to give us clues and glimpses of what is to come. So please do not think I am going to tell you a specific time or date of the Rapture or the Second Coming, which are concealed and hidden from us.

We will, however, know that in the Moedim, God's supernatural timeline connects us to His perfect will and His calendar so that we are not caught unaware and unprepared for what He has promised. If you hear of someone giving you the specifics, most likely they have an agenda that is not in alignment with what this book teaches.

Matthew 24:35-36 NIV
Heaven and earth will pass away, but my words will never pass away. "But about that day or hour no one knows, not even the angels in heaven, nor the Son, but only the Father.

Mark 13:32 NLT
32 "However, no one knows the day or hour when these things will happen, not even the angels in heaven or the Son himself. Only the Father knows.

In these texts Jesus Himself quotes that heaven and earth will pass, but don't ever doubt the validity and authority of His words. We know that Jesus is talking about the last days in both Matthew's and Mark's gospel, but what we do not realize is that He is talking about two different times in the future that He will come or appear again. The first is the gathering of the saints to meet Him in the air like we read in the last chapter in Titus, Corinthians and Thessalonians. He also is talking about another coming, which is His second coming to the earth where His feet touch the Mount of Olives, and will mark the beginning of a thousand year millennial kingdom. The gathering of the saints in the air is what will happen on a future date on the Moedim of Rosh Hashanah, but we do not know precisely when.

Now wait, don't worry, I am not giving you a specific day, only a season to look to. So, let me give you another understanding of why the Jewish people celebrate Rosh Hashanah or the Feast of Trumpets for two days instead of just one.

I have been using the Hebrew term Yom Teruah, but in English we also call it the Feast of Trumpets. Actually, many of the feasts of the Lord will have many names that will help teach us what they mean. This also comes from Scripture. Think of it like titles or names that point to descriptive attributes, like when you are called by a title at work or in your family.

In Judaism the Feast of Trumpets is celebrated for two days and when it starts they will say "NO MAN KNOWETH THE DAY OR THE HOUR". It's rather strange until you realize that this saying is an idiom of their culture.

Rosh Hashanah begins with the sliver of the new moon of the new month and New Year, but back in those days it was almost impossible to predict its beginning and then communicate it to the nation. The lighting of signal fire on the hilltops and mountains would be used to communicate the beginning of the new month. People like the Samaritans would light their own fires to trick Israel into celebrating or starting this Holy time on a day when it had not occurred. This also brought confusion to the people who just wanted to be on God's calendar. This is why they were ready to keep it when they knew it was close, but didn't actually know the day or the hour.

The Rapture of the church will be the same way. We will know it's close as far as the season of the seventh month and physical New Year, but we don't know exactly when that will be.

The Hebrew Calendar is based on the moon, the sun and the agricultural harvest cycle. It is so complicated that Emperor Constantine, being anti-Semitic, had a council and it decided to remove Christianity from the Hebraic calendar. He cited its "complications" as well as the ease of having the Christian holidays now coincide with the pagan culture's already easy to follow calendar and the worship of the sun god, Ra, on what we all call Sunday.

Just because something is not easily understood does not mean we should look for an easier route, for Jeroboam caused Israel to greatly sin by having them worship at a more desirable and closer place and on a day he devised in his own mind. By the way, he also had the people worship golden calves.

I found an article that might help you understand the day a little better.

The Hidden Day
Article by Jason Hommel - "The Feast of Trumpets is
the only festival that no man knows the day or the hour
in which it begins. This is due to the fact that it begins
on the new moon. The new moon was sanctified when
two witnesses see the new moon and attest to it before
the Sanhedrin in the Temple. This sanctification could
happen during either of two days, depending on when
the witnesses come. Since no one knew when the
witnesses would come, no one knew when the Feast of
Trumpets would start. On the 30th of each month, the
members of the High Court assembled in a courtyard in
Jerusalem, where they waited to receive the testimony
of two reliable witnesses. They then sanctified the new
moon. The new moon is very difficult to see on the first
day because it can be seen only about sunset, close to
the sun, when the sun is traveling north. So, looking for
a very slim faint crescent moon, which is very close to
the sun, is a very difficult thing to do. If the moon's
crescent was not seen on the 30th day, the new moon
was automatically celebrated on the 31st day. For this
reason, the Feast of Trumpets is always celebrated for
two days. These two days are celebrated as though it is
just one long day of forty-eight hours. The reason that it
is celebrated for two days is because if they waited to
start the celebration until after the new moon had been
sanctified, they would have missed half the celebration
because the new moon can only be sanctified during
daylight hours. The command seems to be that we
know the season, but not the day or the hour." Another
idiom for the Feast of Trumpets is Yom HaKeseh – the

Hidden Day. Of all the feasts, Yom Teruah is the most mysterious one. There are few scriptures about it. The primary reference is Leviticus 23:23-25. Yom HaKeseh, meaning "The Day of the Hiding" or "the Hidden Day." It is the feast that is concealed as to when it starts. It can only start when the moon begins to reflect again. The New Moon of Tishrei is neither announced nor blessed in the synagogue. The term keseh or keceh is derived from the Hebrew root kacah, which means to "conceal, cover, or hide." Every day during the month of Elul, a trumpet is blown to warn the people to turn back to G-d, except for the last day of Elul, the day preceding Rosh Hashanah (Elul 29 is known as the "Day of Release" at the end of a Shemita year.) On that day, the trumpet is not blown, because it was hidden from Satan, the adversary. It is taught that the Shofar does not blow on this day so that Satan does not know the day judgment begins. Rosh Hashanah is concealed and shrouded in mystery. The mystical aspect of Rosh Hashanah is indicated in Scripture: "Sound the shofar on the New Moon, in concealment of the day of our festival" (Psalm 81:3). The hiddenness of the day also goes along with what Jesus said in Matthew 24 "no man knows the day nor the hour." Psalm 27:5 reminds us: "For in the time of trouble He shall hide me in His pavilion; in the secret of His tabernacle shall He hide me; He shall set me up upon a rock."

Because the gates are understood to be open on Rosh Hashanah, this is further evidence that the

Rapture of the believers in Christ will take place on Rosh Hashanah.

Matthew 24:36-44 NKJV

36 "But of that day and hour no one knows, not even the angels of heaven, but My Father only. 37 But as the days of Noah were, so also will the coming of the Son of Man be. 38 For as in the days before the flood, they were eating and drinking, marrying and giving in marriage, until the day that Noah entered the ark,39 and did not know until the flood came and took them all away, so also will the coming of the Son of Man be. 40 Then two men will be in the field: one will be taken and the other left. 41 Two women will be grinding at the mill: one will be taken and the other left. 42 Watch therefore, for you do not know what hour your Lord is coming. 43 But know this, that if the master of the house had known what hour the thief would come, he would have watched and not allowed his house to be broken into. 44 Therefore you also be ready, for the Son of Man is coming at an hour you do not expect.

Since Rosh Hashanah is the opening of the gates we know that Jesus is speaking prophetically and pointing to the day when He will come and catch away His Bride in the air to be with Him forever. The gates of heaven will open and the righteous ones will enter through them with Jesus.

Isaiah 26:2 NLT
Open the gates to all who are righteous; allow the faithful to enter.

Psalms 118:19-20
19 Open to me the gates of righteousness; I will go through them,
And I will praise the Lord. 20 This is the gate of the Lord, Through which the righteous shall enter.

Ephesians 5:14-17 NKJV
"Awake, sleeper, and arise from the dead, and Christ will shine on you." 15 See then that you walk circumspectly, not as fools but as wise, 16 redeeming the time, because the days are evil. 17 Therefore do not be unwise, but understand what the will of the Lord is.

This Scripture in Ephesians represents the Rapture. The walking in God's ways, His timeline and His Word are the evidence of our righteousness. Don't forget we have positional righteousness because of the Cross, but we must now walk in practical righteousness according to the Torah Word.

"The Resurrection of the Dead" is what we sometimes call "The Rapture."

Psalm 34:19
Many are the afflictions of the righteous, But the Lord delivers him out of them all.

RAPTURE: "rapture" is not found in most Bibles. Greek "harpazo" = "caught up" should have been translated, "to seize, to pluck away; to take by force" but later translated in Latin as "raeptius" or "rapturo".

Hebrew natzal = Lift up, take up, carry; "physically snatch away"

The Rapture is "God judging the righteous." This is when the goats and sheep are separated.

Matthew 24:37-42 TLB
37-38 "The world will be at ease—banquets and parties and weddings—just as it was in Noah's time before the sudden coming of the Flood; 39 people wouldn't believe what was going to happen until the Flood actually arrived and took them all away. So shall my coming be. 40 "Two men will be working together in the fields, and one will be taken, the other left. 41 Two women will be going about their household tasks; one will be taken, the other left. 42 "So be prepared, for you don't know what day your Lord is coming.

If we are found righteous, we leave the earth and get caught away with our bridegroom and heavenly husband. You can see this as prophetic hint with the story of Enoch who is caught away as the 7th generation from Adam.

If we are NOT found righteous; we stay and have seven years to accept Jesus as Messiah during the seven years of the Tribulation. Righteousness is tzedakah in the Hebrew. It means "to do good deeds of charity, kindness and love." We are to live as Jesus' body on this earth. Jesus said many would do works in His name, but He will not acknowledge them because they do not do the will of the Father.

Always remember there are two kinds of righteousness; the positional righteousness when you accept Christ, and the practical righteousness of how you live after you receive Him as your Lord and King of your life. We all need both sides of righteousness the positional by faith and the practical that is walked out by love, obedience and faithfulness by the Holy Spirit. This is a seamless theme in the bible and one that Yeshua-Jesus and the Apostles taught in the Epistles as well.

Matthew 7:21
"Not everyone who says to Me, 'Lord, Lord,' shall enter the kingdom of heaven, but he who does the will of My Father in heaven.

Now please remember that when you name the Name of the Lord you will depart from evil. Also always remember that the Rapture is different and separate from the Second Coming of Christ. In the Rapture we will meet Jesus in the air, but during His second coming His feet will touch the earth. We want to be counted worthy go in the Rapture. For if we are not found righteous in the way we have been living, it will be because we have not received the teaching as the

Scriptures have been instructing us and we won't be a Bride that is awake and ready for her Husband.

God has given us His Torah instruction so we "Hit the Mark" and are ready when He comes. We have to walk in the abundant life Jesus came to give us and the blessings will overtake us.

The Hebrew Wedding Ceremony:
"Kiddushin/Nesu'in"

The Rapture is when the Bride of Christ is caught up to heaven to be wed and a consummation of marriage with the Groom, Jesus will occur. The Rapture or the catching away is a marital term, and in the Hebrew wedding we can see a type and shadow present.

In the ancient Hebrew wedding ceremony, the groom comes for his bride without warning to take (seize/rapture/natzal) her away to the bridal chamber. The marriage takes place over a period of time known as the "bridal week". During the bridal week, for seven days, the groom and bride have intimacy and relations in the bridal chamber. At the end of the week, the bride & groom emerge from the wedding chamber and there's a marriage supper.

The seven-day period can also refer to seven years of what we call the Tribulation period or the time of Jacob's trouble. The righteous church will be caught away in heaven with the Lord and won't have to go through the Tribulation. We can see this in the book of

Daniel, whom Jesus also gleaned from what He said in the book of Matthew.

Daniel 12:1-4 (NASB)
"Now at that time Michael, the great prince (angel) who stands guard over the sons of your people, will arise. And there will be a time of distress such as never occurred since there was a nation until that time; and at that time (when Michael arises) your people, everyone who is found written in the book, will be rescued. (from the Tribulation) 2 Many of those who sleep in the dust of the ground will awake, these to everlasting life, but the others to disgrace and everlasting contempt. 3 Those who have insight (on alert and watch for it) will shine brightly like the brightness of the expanse of heaven, and those who lead the many to righteousness, (tzedakah) like the stars forever and ever. 4 But as for you, Daniel, conceal these words and seal up the book until the end of time;

So, since Jesus was referring to the Rapture in the Scriptures we read, we must also realize that His discourse did not end there. He knows each Moedim is prophetic and points to many things in the future.

The tenth day of the seventh month is known as the holiest day of the year for Israel. This is what we call the Day of Atonement. Let's look at what it means and why we still should and get to keep it today as Christians.

I like to say about all of God's Moedim and Word, it's not that we have to, but we get to! As you continue, keep that in mind. We don't serve God out of the letter of the law, but the Holy Spirit that works God's good pleasure in us. His Moedim are Divine Appointments and are invitations for you and all His people to come up higher and to be with Him. You are never being forced or coerced, but invited as a son or daughter to come to the King's table. Like King David because of covenant relationship He invites Mephibosheth the son of Johnathan to be carried to His table and abide continually in his presence and provides abundantly for him. Yeshua- Jesus does the same thing for us as He carries those who are dependent on Him to the place of abundance and favor.

CHAPTER THREE:

Personal and Small Group Study

The Word of God and the _________________ are part of the _________ of heaven and is a part of the way the Holy Spirit will use to ___________ us on our journey as He uses them to give us _____________ and _______________ of what is to come.

God's supernatural timeline _________________ us to His perfect will and His _________________ so that we are not caught unaware and _______________for what He has promised.

What two events is Jesus talking about in Mathew's and Mark's gospel that will occur in the future?

____

____

____

____

____

____

____

____

Matthew 24:35-36 NIV
Heaven and earth will pass away, but my ____________
will never pass away. "But about that day or
__________________ no one ______________, not
even the angels in heaven, nor the Son, but only the
____________.

Since Rosh Hashanah is the opening of the
____________ we know that Jesus is speaking
______________________ and pointing to the day when
He will come and ________ away His ____________
in the air to be with Him forever.

What saying of Jesus is a Jewish Idiom?

____

____

____

Isaiah 26:2 NLT

Open the gates to all who are ______________; allow the faithful to enter.

The ___________ of heaven will open and the __________________ ones will enter through them with Jesus.

The _____________ is when the Bride of Christ is _____________ up to heaven to be wed and a consummation of ________________ with the Groom, Jesus will occur.

The seven-day period can also refer to seven years of what we call the ___________________ period or the time of _______________ trouble.

In the _______________ we will meet Jesus in the __________, but during His second coming His __________will touch the earth.

The _____________________ church will be caught away in __________________ with the Lord and won't have to go through the ___________________.

Describe what is "the Hidden Day" in Rosh Hashanah.

____

____

____

____

____

CHAPTER FOUR:

Day of Atonement

I hope you are beginning to see how God's Moedim are appointments, invitations and rehearsals so we are ready for what is to come. They are part of His rhythm and His cycles of growing His people to become more like Jesus. The physical world and what we do both teach us about spiritual truths and connect us to them as we walk it out in this natural world.

1 Corinthians 15:46
46 However, the spiritual is not first, but the natural, and afterward the spiritual.

As you walk by faith and in the timeline of heaven here on earth, you will be opened up to the blessings God has for you. The natural realm and the keeping of the Moedim are connecting you to their realities in heaven. We know that the heavenly Jerusalem is our mother, yet it is not seen from this realm. We connect to it as we continue to walk as He walked.

Ten days after Feast of Trumpets is Yom Kippur, which is also called the Day of Atonement. This was only time of year when the high priest went into the Holy of Holies to make atonement for his sins and for the people.

Let's read about it in the Scriptures.

Leviticus 17:11
11 For the life of the flesh is in the blood, and I have given it to you upon the altar to make atonement for your souls; for it is the blood that makes atonement for the soul.

Hebrews 9:7 NKJV
7 But into the second part the high priest went alone once a year, not without blood, which he offered for himself and for the people's sins committed in ignorance;

We know ultimately it will be the blood of Messiah, the Lamb of God that will be received by God as the atonement for our souls. The price of redemption is costly and because of Jesus we are saved by grace through faith and it is a gift. Now that we have received such a wonderful gift, we give the gift of our lives back to God as a living sacrifice, willing to do whatever He desires or asks.

Leviticus 23:26-32 NKJV
26 And the Lord spoke to Moses, saying: 27 "Also the tenth day of this seventh month shall be the Day of Atonement. It shall be a holy convocation for you; you shall afflict your souls, and offer an offering made by fire to the Lord. 28 And you shall do no work on that same day, for it is the Day of Atonement, to make atonement for you before the Lord your God. 29 For any person who is not afflicted in soul on that same day shall be cut off from his people. 30 And any person who does any work on that same day, that person I will destroy from among his people. 31 You shall do no manner of work; it shall be a statute forever throughout your generations in all your dwellings. 32 It shall be to you a sabbath of solemn rest, and you shall afflict your souls; on the ninth day of the month at evening, from evening to evening, you shall celebrate your sabbath."

So we see something very significant here. The only time in the Bible that God wants His people to afflict their souls is during this solemn day. Since most every feast day is a party, this will be an exception, for this day you will search your heart and life for any unconfessed, un-repented sin. There are three types of sin you will want to deal with; the sins of commission, sins of omission and sins of ignorance.

During the year Israel would go three times to Jerusalem to keep the Chagag, which were the feasts that required them to be present and offer sacrifices. The Day of Atonement differs because it has to do with covering the gap of the sins you might have missed along the way. The Day of Atonement, when kept, assured you that you were ready for Judgment Day because those sins that might have gone unaware have now been covered on this day.

The word atonement means "to cover" and is not a word found in the New Testament because Jesus didn't just "cover" or "atone" for our sins, He remitted and removed them completely. This does not mean we won't benefit from keeping this day, for we too have times when sin has caught us unaware by omission, commission and ignorance. The blessing we connect with is one of alignment and drawing closer to God during this invitation and divine appointment.

For years as a young observant Jewish boy I would go to temple on this most holy day and do my fasting. I didn't know that God had commanded this as the only day of required fasting as an affliction of the soul. Fasting does not save you or make you more holy. It is, however a way to deny the physical flesh and the outer man control of your life. It lets our flesh know that the Holy Spirit and inner man has dominance in our life and not the lower desires of our human nature.

Isaiah 58:5-14 NKJV
5 Is it a fast that I have chosen, A day for a man to afflict his soul? Is it to bow down his head like a bulrush, And to spread out sackcloth and ashes?

Would you call this a fast, And an acceptable day to the
Lord? 6 "Is this not the fast that I have chosen: To loose
the bonds of wickedness, To undo the heavy burdens,
To let the oppressed go free, And that you break every
yoke? 7 Is it not to share your bread with the hungry,
And that you bring to your house the poor who are cast
out; When you see the naked, that you cover him,
And not hide yourself from your own flesh?
8 Then your light shall break forth like the morning,
Your healing shall spring forth speedily,
And your righteousness shall go before you;
The glory of the Lord shall be your rear guard.
9 Then you shall call, and the Lord will answer;
You shall cry, and He will say, 'Here I am.'
"If you take away the yoke from your midst,
The pointing of the finger, and speaking wickedness,
10 If you extend your soul to the hungry
And satisfy the afflicted soul, Then your light shall
dawn in the darkness, And your darkness shall be as the
noonday. 11 The Lord will guide you continually,
And satisfy your soul in drought, And strengthen your
bones; You shall be like a watered garden,
And like a spring of water, whose waters do not fail.
12 Those from among you Shall build the old waste
places; You shall raise up the foundations of many
generations; And you shall be called the Repairer of the
Breach, The Restorer of Streets to Dwell In.
13 "If you turn away your foot from the Sabbath, From
doing your pleasure on My holy day, And call the
Sabbath a delight, The holy day of the Lord honorable,
And shall honor Him, not doing your own ways,

Nor finding your own pleasure, Nor speaking your own words, 14 Then you shall delight yourself in the Lord; And I will cause you to ride on the high hills of the earth, And feed you with the heritage of Jacob your father. The mouth of the Lord has spoken."

The blessings of fasting and keeping the Day of Atonement are concealed for us in this chapter of Isaiah. So many blessings! Through the power of the fast on the Day of Atonement, as you afflict yourself, God has promised to show up and show off in you and through you, causing you to be a blessing to those who are hurting. You will be a light, the way Jesus told us to be, when we fast and keep this appointed day. Look at all the blessings the fast on this day promises to us.

LOOSE THE BONDS OF WICKEDNESS

UNDO HEAVY BURDENS

SETTING THE OPPRESSED FREE

BREAKING THE BONDAGES AND YOKES OFF THE PEOPLE

FEEDING THE HUNGRY WITH BREAD

TAKING CARE OF THE POOR AND THOSE CAST ASIDE

COVERING THE NAKED

BEING A LIGHT TO THE DARKNESS

SPEEDY HEALING FOR OUR PHYSICAL BODIES

RIGHTEOUSNESS MAKING A PATH BEFORE US

THE GLORY OF GOD GUARDING OUR REAR

ANSWERS TO OUR PRAYERS

So many blessing that it's hard to count them all and they overflow to those who need them most. I have listed twelve of these blessings and promises of fasting on the Day of Atonement, but you can probably find many more! This is why we get to keep the special day, and if you do, you will see the fruit in your life, family and the world around you.

Did you know there are three types of **"Trumps"** in the Bible? I am talking about the blowing of the shofar or trumpet. The Jewish people today know about these times, but because we have been disconnected from the roots of the faith we have lost many blessings and revelations that have already been revealed to the Hebrew people who have been keeping the appointed times knowing they have a deeper meaning. Since the time of Yeshua many of these hidden mysteries have come to bring light not just to the Jew, but also to those who have been grafted in and are connected by the root to the stock and blessing of Abraham. Each and every Appointed Feast day when walked out will bring new understanding and revealing of Christ in a more complete way. You will truly go from glory to glory for it never really ends.

First Trump: On Pentecost as the betrothal of marriage (Exodus 19:19)

Last Trump: On Rosh Hashanah as the consummation of marriage (Leviticus 23:23)

Great Trump: On Day of Atonement pointing to the Second Coming and judgment seat of Christ (2 Corinthians 5:10)

Once you understand these three trumpets the New Testament writings will become revealed through what had been concealed in what we call the Old Covenant Scriptures.

Matthew 24:31
31 And He will send His angels with a great sound of a trumpet, and they will gather together His elect from the four winds, from one end of heaven to the other.

Zechariah 14:4
4 And in that day His feet will stand on the Mount of Olives, Which faces Jerusalem on the east. And the Mount of Olives shall be split in two,

From east to west, Making a very large valley; Half of the mountain shall move toward the north And half of it toward the south.

The Day of Atonement is a day the rabbis believe that one day in the future God will judge the entire world. We know we will stand before the judgment seat, but for the saints it will not be about heaven or hell, for that has already been settled for believers. The judgment for the saints has to do with whether or not we have done what was written compared to the book and plan God had for us from the beginning. We came to earth on a mission from God with an assignment, calling and the gifts and resources to do what was written about us in heaven before we were born.

Psalm 139:16
Your eyes saw my substance, being yet unformed. And in Your book they all were written, The days fashioned for me, When as yet there were none of them

Revelation 20:12
12 And I saw the dead, small and great, standing before God, and books were opened. And another book was opened, which is the Book of Life. And the dead were judged according to their works, by the things, which were written in the books.

Many of you might be familiar with the teaching on how you have a book in heaven about you and how God wants you to walk in the fullness of what He has written and planned for you. When you and I stand before God, the book of your life will be opened and you will be judged according to your works by the things that were written in your book. This is not a heaven or hell issue, but rather a destiny and purpose one. The heart of God and why it is important to keep these specific appointed days is because they actually will help you sync to God's calendar and timeline, thus recalibrating your life to what is in your book! Our practical righteousness is walking in all the good things He has planned for us to walk in and enjoy.

So what will happen on the Day of Judgment? Let's look at the words of Jesus.

Matthew 25:31-46 NKJV
31 "When the Son of Man comes in His glory, and all the holy angels with Him, then He will sit on the throne of His glory. 32 All the nations will be gathered before Him, and He will separate them one from another, as a shepherd divides his sheep from the goats. 33 And He will set the sheep on His right hand, but the goats on the left. 34 Then the King will say to those on His right hand, 'Come, you blessed of My Father, inherit the kingdom prepared for you from the foundation of the world:35 for I was hungry and you gave Me food; I was thirsty and you gave Me drink; I was a stranger and you took Me in; 36 I was naked and you clothed Me; I was sick and you visited Me; I was in prison and you came to Me.'

37 "Then the righteous will answer Him, saying, 'Lord, when did we see You hungry and feed You, or thirsty and give You drink? 38 When did we see You a stranger and take You in, or naked and clothe You? 39 Or when did we see You sick, or in prison, and come to You?' 40 And the King will answer and say to them, 'Assuredly, I say to you, inasmuch as you did it to one of the least of these My brethren, you did it to Me.'
41 "Then He will also say to those on the left hand, 'Depart from Me, you cursed, into the everlasting fire prepared for the devil and his angels: 42 for I was hungry and you gave Me no food; I was thirsty and you gave Me no drink; 43 I was a stranger and you did not take Me in, naked and you did not clothe Me, sick and in prison and you did not visit Me.'
44 "Then they also will answer Him, saying, 'Lord, when did we see You hungry or thirsty or a stranger or naked or sick or in prison, and did not minister to You?'45 Then He will answer them, saying, 'Assuredly, I say to you, inasmuch as you did not do it to one of the least of these, you did not do it to Me.' 46 And these will go away into everlasting punishment, but the righteous into eternal life."

In this passage Jesus is talking about a day in the future in which He will judge all the nations. This judgment will be about righteousness and doing what God required in His Word. The sheep will be the humble committed followers of God and His instructions, while the goats will be those who refused to hear and obey. The sheep will have no fear of punishment for they will enter into eternal life as a reward. The nations who did not accept the Lord and His ways will be sent to everlasting punishment.

The unrighteous on the Day of Atonement will be blotted out of the Book of Life forever if they have refused to repent. It is God's goodness that leads to repentance and it is a gift according to Romans 2:4.

The grace and mercy of God extends to all, but it must be received humbly in order for the grace not to be repelled by human pride. On this same Day of Atonement, the righteous ones will be forever sealed and written in God's Book of Life. They will enter into glory forever to be with the Husband and Groom, Jesus. Those who have not had the gap of sin closed and have not heeded the warnings will lose the reward that God wants to give them, but cannot.

1 Peter 4:17-19 NKJV
17 For the time has come for judgment to begin at the house of God; and if it begins with us first, what will be the end of those who do not obey the gospel of God? 18 Now "If the righteous one is scarcely saved, Where will the ungodly and the sinner appear?" 19 Therefore let those who suffer according to the will of God commit their souls to Him in doing good, as to a faithful Creator.

1 Corinthians 3:11-15 NKJV

11 For no other foundation can anyone lay than that which is laid, which is Jesus Christ. 12 Now if anyone builds on this foundation with gold, silver, precious stones, wood, hay, straw, 13 each one's work will become clear; for the Day will declare it, because it will be revealed by fire; and the fire will test each one's work, of what sort it is. 14 If anyone's work which he has built on it endures, he will receive a reward. 15 If anyone's work is burned, he will suffer loss; but he himself will be saved, yet so as through fire.

The judgment for the saints will not be heaven or hell, but on what have we done. God is looking for our practical righteousness so that we live in the ways and instructions He has given us. Being a light requires that we walk in the truth. We will be judged for how we have done what was expected as good and faithful servants. Our relationship with God is as a son or daughter and also a Bride. Each one has responsibilities that come from a heart of love. We don't do things to be saved; however, we will do, out of love, many things because we have been saved.

The husband for example will do what is best for the family, not because he is commanded to, but because he honors and values the relationship and gift that was given by God's grace. Grace and obedience are really two sides of one coin. The order is always to receive by grace through faith first, then you will walk in obedience by faith because of the love you have for

Jesus. In the book of John our Lord said, "If you love Me you will keep My commands." John 14:15

The Day of Atonement is a revelation of the final judgment to come and the Second Coming of Christ to the earth. As we celebrate this feast as Christians, we are reminded of the atoning work of Christ and our part in walking in the light of His Torah instructions. The rewards will await us as we keep these special days… because we get to!

Revelation 17:14
14 These will make war with the Lamb, and the Lamb will overcome them, for He is Lord of lords and King of kings; and those who are with Him are called, chosen, and faithful."

CHAPTER FOUR:

Personal and Small Group Study

The ____________________world and what we do both
teach us about ______________________truths and
connect us to them as we walk it out in this
____________________ world.

1 Corinthians 15:46
46 However, the ____________________ is not first, but
the ____________________, and afterward the
____________________.

____________________ days after Feast of Trumpets is
________ ____________, which is also called the Day of
____________________. This is only time of year when
the high priest goes into the Holy of Holies to make
____________________for his sins and for the people.

_____________________ does not save you or make you
more _______________. It is however a way to deny
the _______________ flesh and the outer man
_______________ of your life.

What does it mean to afflict your souls?

____

____

List the twelve blessings of fasting on the Day of
Atonement.
1.____

____

2.____

____

3.____

____

4.____

____

5.____

____

6.____

____

7.____

____

8.____

____

9.____

____

10.____

____
11.____

____
12.____

____

The three specific Trumps in the Bible are:

________________ Trump: On ____________ as the
________________ of marriage (Exodus 19:19)

________________ Trump: On _______________
as the ______________ of marriage (Leviticus 23:23)

________________ Trump: On
__________________________pointing to the
________________coming and ________________ seat
of Christ. (2 Corinthians 5:10)

When you and I stand before God, the book of your life
will be __________ and you will be
________________according to your works by the
things that were __________________ in your
______________.

According to 1 Peter chapter four, where does judgment
begin?

Revelation 20:12

12 And I saw the dead, small and great, standing before
God, and _____________________ were opened. And
another book was opened, which is the Book of Life.
And the dead were _________________ according to
their works, by the things, which were
_________________ in the _________________.
The _____________________ on the Day of Atonement
will be _____________ out of the Book of Life forever
if they have refused to repent.

God is looking for our _________________
righteousness so that we live in the ways and
_________________ He has given us.

1 Corinthians 3:14-15

14 If anyone's _________ which he has built on it
_____________, he will receive a reward. 15 If anyone's
work is burned, he will _________ loss; but he
himself will be _________, yet so as through
_____________.

Revelation 17:14
14 These will make war with the Lamb, and the Lamb will overcome them, for He is Lord of lords and King of kings; and those who are with Him are

____________, ________________, and
________________ ”

About the Author

Kenneth "Ken" Albin was born in New York, but moved to Florida as a young seven-year-old. Shortly after moving, Ken's parents were divorced, which left him deeply hurt for many years. During this time Ken, being Jewish, went to Hebrew school and Temple regularly. At the time of his thirteenth birthday and Bar Mitzvah, many confirmed a calling as a "rabbi" or "cantor" on his life.

It was soon after this that Ken's grandparents met the Lord at a Full Gospel businessmen's meeting. With momentum that came from above, Ken's father, David accepted the Lord, Jesus as his Savior. Being moved by his father's "born again" experience, Ken was now himself open to hear the message that so radically changed his dad's life. In the summer of Ken's sophomore year of high school, he gave his life to Jesus and his life was radically altered. He has been faithful to the house of God ever since. His mother, Racquel had also accepted Jesus and was now serving the Lord full time in Messianic ministry with her new husband, Rabbi Charles Kluge.

Ken has served in various areas of ministry including children's ministry, youth ministry and music ministry. He also has served in both associate and senior pastor roles for over twenty years. He has earned his Bachelor of Theology from International Seminary and his Master's Degree from Liberty University. He is also an accomplished singer/songwriter who has written over 100 songs. He loves to worship with the guitar and the keyboard.

Ken met his wife, Lisa at her grandfather's church in Margate, Florida. They were married when Lisa was just eighteen years of age. Six years later they welcomed their only child, Brittney into the world. Today Brittney and her husband, A.J. serve with Ken and Lisa in ministry and have a beautiful daughter, Brielle.

Ken and Lisa founded Save the Nations Church along with a handful of committed people who gathered in a home on September 17, 2006. God had put a vision in their hearts to reach the nations and bring light to a hurting world. Ken and Lisa currently serve as the overseeing pastors of the South Florida church campus in Broward County. As founders and pastors, they desire to inspire, instruct, resource and help people discover the destiny God has for them. The nations have become their home as together they travel to the nations, teaching, reviving and sharing the resources that help make influential disciples and bring people into appreciation of God's Torah, His "instructions."

Ken has always preached the word with the inspiration and revelation of the Holy Spirit. He has recently been on a journey to bring Christians into an understanding of the roots of their faith. "The Christian church has been hacked!" as Ken states in one of his latest books about restoring the inheritance and identity back to the church.

Presently, there are two international Save the Nations churches in Brazil: one in Rio and one in Marica'. Brazilian pastors, Diego and Kelly are doing an amazing work for God and great fruit is seen in that nation.

Ken has authored many books. All are available on Amazon. They are also being translated to Spanish, Portuguese and Russian languages.

Ways you can connect with Kenneth Albin through social media. www.hitthemarktorah.tv

BOOKS BY KENNETH S. ALBIN

YOU ARE BORN FOR THE EXTRAORDINARY

UPSIDE OF DOWN

THE MYSTERY OF THE CROWN

HACKED: THE HEBREW CHRISTIAN

THE PASSOVER BLESSING

NO MORE LEAVEN

HIT THE MARK

CELEBRATE TABERNACLES

HANUKKAH AND PURIM ARE FOR CHRISTIANS TOO

THE BLESSINGS OF PENTECOST

Contact Information: for Ken & Lisa Albin
 www.savethenations.com / www.hitthemarktv.com
info@savethenations.com

THE BLESSINGS OF PENTECOST

KENNETH S. ALBIN

KENNETH S. ALBIN

Tabernacles
It's a Celebration
& Not Just
an Option

How Christians can celebrate this
Biblical Feast and the True Birthday of Messiah

Christians

GET TO CELEBRATE

Passover

TOO!

Learning its Secrets, Power and Abundant Blessings

KENNETH S. ALBIN

REVEALED

A Christian Understanding for Celebrating
the Biblical Holidays of Rosh Hashanah and Yom Kippur

BY KENNETH S. ALBIN

HIT THE MARK

How Christians can
walk in the mysteries
of the Torah

And receive
all its blessings

Kenneth S. Albin

HACKED
פריצה
זהרת
RESTORING
STOLEN IDENTITY
AND EMBRACING THE
INHERITED BLESSING
THE HEBREW
CHRISTIAN

THE MYSTERY

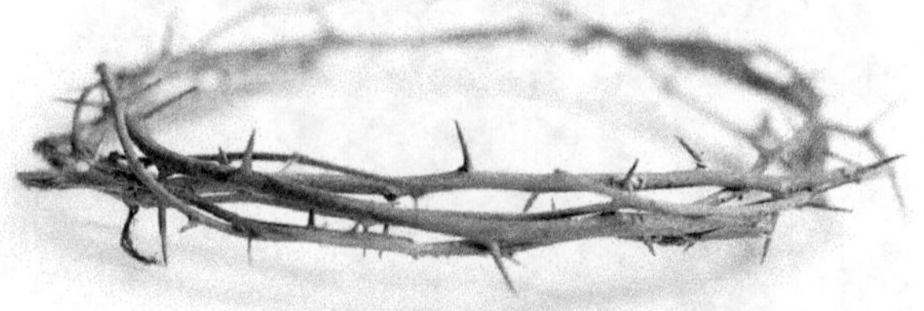

OF THE CROWN

"WHY CHRIST HAD TO RECEIVE IT &
HOW ITS SECRETS CAN CHANGE YOUR WORLD."

FOREWORD BY TED SHUTTLESWORTH

KENNETH STEVEN ALBIN

YOU ARE BORN FOR THE
EXTRAORDINARY
FOREWORD BY DR. SAMUEL CHAND

DISCOVER YOUR GREATER PURPOSE
AND WALK IN THE BOOK WRITTEN OF YOUR LIFE

HOW INTENTIONALLY GOING LOWER CAN TAKE YOU HIGHER

UPSIDE OF DOWN

FOREWORD BY
DR. MARK
CHIRONNA

KENNETH S. ALBIN

HACKEADO

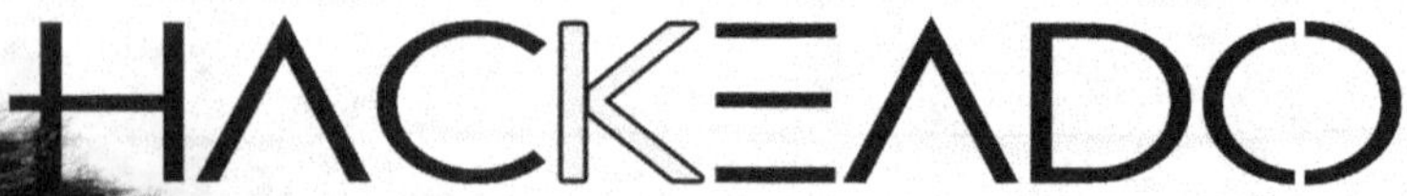

פריצה

RESTAURANDO
A IDENTIDADE
ROUBADA E
ADOTANDO A
BENÇÃO HERDADA

O HEBREU CRISTÃO

HANUKKAH
and PURIM
ARE FOR CHRISTIANS TOO!

KENNETH S. ALBIN

KENNETH STEVEN ALBIN

VOCÊ NASCEU PARA O
EXTRAORDINÁRIO

PREFÁCIO DE DR. SAMUEL CHAND

AS OITO CHAVES QUE REVELAM
O EXTRAORDINÁRIO DENTRO DE VOCÊ

APRENDA A VIVER HUMILDEMENTE PARA SER EXALTADO

DE CABEÇA PARA BAIXO

PREFÁCIO POR
DR. MARK CHIRONNA

KENNETH S. ALBIN

КАК, ОПУСКАЯСЬ ВНИЗ, ПОДНИМАТЬСЯ ВЫШЕ!

СНИЗУ ВВЕРХ

ПРЕДИСЛОВИЕ Д-РА МАРКА ЧИРОННЫ

КЕННЕТ С. АЛБИН